EVEN
THE
DEMONS
BELIEVE

EVEN
THE
DEMONS
BELIEVE

*You believe that there is one
God. Good! Even the demons
believe that—and shudder.*
(*James 2:19*)

TIMOTHY WILLIAMS

CARRIED CROSS
BOOKS

© 2001 by Timothy Williams.
All rights reserved.
First edition printed January 2001
Second edition printed July 2001
Third edition printed January 2003
Fourth edition printed October 2005

Published by Carried Cross Books,
PO Box 856, Enumclaw, WA 98022.

Unless otherwise noted, all scriptures are taken from the Holy Bible, New International Version, Copyright © 1973, 1978, 1984 by the International Bible Society. Used by permission of Zondervan Publishing House. The "NIV" and "New International Version" trademarks are registered in the United States Patent and Trademark Office by International Bible Society.

ISBN 1-57921-355-3
Library of Congress Catalog Card Number: 00-111854

Cover design by His Workmanship

Dedicated to all who love God enough to reject cheap grace.

Again, the kingdom of heaven is like a merchant looking for fine pearls. When he found one of great value, he went away and sold everything he had and bought it.

(Matthew 13:45–46)

CONTENTS

Foreword 9

Assumption 13

CHAPTER 1
    Which Way to Salvation? 15
CHAPTER 2
    Even Demons Believe in God 23
CHAPTER 3
    Large Crowds Traveling with Jesus 31
CHAPTER 4
    Christian or Disciple?....................................39
CHAPTER 5
    First Sit Down 47
CHAPTER 6
    God's Terms of Peace 55
CHAPTER 7
    Losing Our Saltiness.......................................63

CHAPTER 8
  Shaking the Salt Shaker 69
CHAPTER 9
  Why the Cross? 83
CHAPTER 10
  The First Sermon 91
CHAPTER 11
  The Full Message 101
CHAPTER 12
  Giving Orders 111
CHAPTER 13
  A Daily Cross 119
CHAPTER 14
  Having This Attitude 127
CHAPTER 15
  Re-Baptized 135
CHAPTER 16
  The Joy 145
CHAPTER 17
  Why Become a Christian? 155
CHAPTER 18
  Feelings 165
CHAPTER 19
  The First Step of Humility 173

Everything Said 181

Endnotes 183

Request Discipleship 191

FOREWORD

As you open this book, my wife and I would like to share our experiences in both extremes of Christianity, from cheap grace to legalistic. I personally grew up in the charismatic church and now, looking back, I am amazed at the things I believed. How could I look at Jesus' life and think it was so easy to follow Him? Most Sunday messages consisted of stories, jokes, or experiences of the pastor, yet held no power. It was like going to children's church for adults. At the conclusion of every sermon, and after the moral of the story was revealed, everyone bowed their heads. The Pastor would then ask if anyone wanted to be saved or felt a tugging at their hearts to raise their hands, repeat a prayer, and instantly receive salvation. I did that. I can't count how many times I raised my hand, yet it never caused my heart to change. No one ever told me how to count the cost of following Christ. I could keep sinning and still be covered by God's "grace," but never change. I didn't know what it meant to be a disciple and certainly no one ever warned me of the cost. My wife tells a different story.

———————

Growing up I (Jessica) had very little experience with church. When Greg and I met, neither of us walked with the Lord. Then right before we married, I started searching for a church. A friend told me of a small non-denominational church that seemed to preach the truth. Greg and I began to attend there regularly. Since my life was ridden with sin, I felt convicted every time I heard a sermon. At this church, I saw a lot of things in me that needed to change and was taught that if the Bible says it, you do it. After time, however, my heart started to feel heavier and heavier as if I was dying a very slow death. I found it impossible to do what the scriptures and sermons said. This confused me deeply. My relationships with people at church grew colder and colder. I began to cry out to God to show me what I was doing wrong. I wanted to change and obey Him, but my Christianity was powerless. The church leaders concluded that I struggled because I hadn't gone up to the altar and asked Jesus into my heart, even though they had baptized me. The more I questioned and asked for guidance, the more they placed legalistic rules on me. Eventually, they asked me to leave and not come back. Finally, Greg and I saw the deception of the church's controlling rules and left.

———————

Neither Jessica or myself (Greg) wanted to run from God, but with my liberal past and now this experience, we grew more and more confused. The passage about walking the narrow road plagued Jessica, but we had no idea where to find it. At the end of our rope, the Lord revealed to us a Christianity with power, the message of the cross.

One day Jessica caught the tale end of a radio program and checked the web site given by the author of this book. The teaching sounded much like what we had just left, yet we sensed something different. We felt God's love and strength in the message. It seemed to balance receiving God's grace with denying ourselves. This message gave us hope because we learned that we could change by God's power.

Coming from the "we are free to do whatever and covered by the blood" to the "if the Bible says it, do it" extremes, we felt hungry and unsatisfied. On hearing the message of the cross we became full of joy, yet at the same time overwhelmed with the power and love of God. My wife and I had no idea the life changing experience that God would bring. No longer did we walk on a wide path leading to cheap, easy grace. We discovered that God's grace teaches us to say "No" to sin and pride. Jessica found that she could be accepted by God and walk and change by the power of the Spirit. The message of the cross is no easy believism, nor is it harsh legalism.

While reading this you might say, "This can't be right" or maybe you will fall on your face before God as we did. Please do not take counting the cost lightly. The cross has brought us extreme joy and at the same time overwhelming helplessness, knowing that we can do nothing without Jesus, which is exactly where God wants us to be.

In some ways, this message felt harder than the one before, because at the cross our deepest sins are revealed. God's love seems unbearable at times because for our benefit He disciplines us. At the cross, however, Jessica and I began to work out our own salvation with fear and trembling. There we have found joy in our marriage and a relationship with the Lord that we never experienced before. It's not enough to walk by the rules laid down by God in the Bible—true salvation comes by doing it solely by His power. And it's not enough to quickly accept His grace and say we believe in God—because even the demons believe.

Greg & Jessica Gambill

ASSUMPTION

It is assumed that the reader understands Jesus took our punishment for sins when He died on the cross.[1] By this act of mercy we now have the opportunity to become disciples of Jesus and live for righteousness. Christ opened for us the way to salvation and fellowship with the living God. Everything you are about to read points to entering through the narrow gate by way of the anointing sacrifice performed by Jesus on the cross.

> Therefore, brothers, since we have confidence to enter the Most Holy Place by the blood of Jesus, by a new and living way opened for us through the curtain, that is, his body, and since we have a great priest over the house of God, let us draw near to God with a sincere heart in full assurance of faith, having our hearts sprinkled to cleanse us

from a guilty conscience and having our bodies washed with pure water. (Hebrews 10:19-22)

Praise God for His rich mercy! The way has been "opened" and so let us with humble hearts discover how we too may find "confidence to enter the Most Holy Place by the blood of Jesus."

CHAPTER 1

Which Way to Salvation?

This is what the Lord says: "Stand at the crossroads and look; ask for the ancient paths, ask where the good way is, and walk in it, and you will find rest for your souls . . ." (Jeremiah 6:16)

Every church has their method for getting to heaven, so how can a person know the correct path? With all the different beliefs and opinions about what it means to be a Christian, no wonder so many people feel thoroughly confused.[2] In fact, many have given up the search for God altogether because the task to discover the truth seems too overwhelming. Additionally, many today falsely think that opinion equals belief, and if we think something sincerely enough, God will accept us. To further compound the problem, multitudes of hypocritical "Christians" claim they know God. All of these things and more frustrate those with an honest search for God.

To find the answers, we need to follow Jeremiah's direction: "Ask for the ancient paths, ask where the good way is" and then "walk in it." Through these God-given words we will find "rest for" our "souls."

In Luke 7:48 Jesus told a woman, "Your sins are forgiven." God forgave every wrong thing in her actions and thoughts. Those words are the sweetest words a man or woman can ever hear.

God's forgiveness should set us free and light our hearts aflame with an undying love for Him.[3] In order to hear those words, we must first consider what it means to be a Christian. Otherwise, we place ourselves in danger of being "denounced" by the very God who touches our lives with love and power.[4] As the following Scripture demonstrates, Jesus disowned those whom God had touched in a powerful way because they would not "repent." With this in mind, let us look at what it really means to be a Christian, how one becomes a Christian, and the requirements to keep from being "denounce[d]" by God. In short, let us see the truth according to Jesus.

> Then Jesus began to denounce the cities in which most of his miracles had been performed, because they did not repent.
> (Matthew 11:20)

When Jesus walked on the earth, He made Christians in a very odd fashion. Jesus won souls, as we shall see, in a manner that may surprise most.[5] This book examines how someone becomes a Christian according to Jesus.

Most individuals, who consider themselves Christians, have responded to God's love in a way that would not receive Jesus' approval. As Paul stated in the book of Romans, they did not "submit" to God's way of salvation and instead "sought to establish their own."

> Since they did not know the righteousness that comes from God and sought to establish their own, they did not submit to God's righteousness. (Romans 10:3)

Every church and denomination has their methods for saving individuals. Each has "established their own" way of salvation. But God declared long ago that only "one" way leads to heaven.

> . . . one Lord, one faith, one baptism . . . (Ephesians 4:5)

Each man must make a decision to either submit to God's righteousness or embrace man's religious ways. God's righteousness grows eternally, but the peace and security of man offers only empty hope.

In the church today, we have established many different ways to become a Christian. People can come forward after a sermon, raise their hands, attend classes, speak in tongues, or repeat the words someone tells them to say. The salvation calls, coming forward to accept Jesus, vary from church to church, but which one is of God? Let us go back and look at how Jesus made someone a Christian. We will look at Jesus' salvation call,[6] and if it does not match up to ours, let us repent and "submit to God's righteousness."

Truths to Ponder, Beliefs to Examine

- What opinions do you hold about the way of salvation?

- Why do you hold these opinions? Where did you learn them?

- If you submit to God's righteousness, what might happen to these beliefs?

- Are you ready to examine your beliefs deeper?

1 Believe in God, infant baptism
Later I learned Jesus came
down from heaven to die on the
cross for our sins so we may have
eternal life.

2 I was taught them as an
adult in a Lutheran church.
1st 2 as a child - same church

3 I believe in the third one

4. yes

CHAPTER 2

Even Demons Believe in God

Most believe in God and the vast majority of the world is religious. Even those who do not believe in God have faith in their belief that there is no God. Those without a specific belief foolishly believe in themselves.[7] Therefore, it is safe to say every man believes in something. Believing comes easy to man, because God has given him this ability.[8] Unfortunately, man has invented many things to believe in. The number of "schemes" man creates in order to satisfy his desires to believe are indeed "many."

> This only have I found: God made mankind upright, but men have gone in search of many schemes. (Ecclesiastes 7:29)

Christianity is no exception. The Christian church searched out and created many different "schemes" to get to Jesus. Those "schemes" range from just asking Jesus into your heart, speaking in tongues, signing the back of a Bible, saying the Rosary, to being water baptized. Let us return to the path Jesus set down and accept His instructions for belief in God.

"If anyone comes to me . . ." (Luke 14:26)

"If anyone comes to" Jesus for salvation, he must understand specific things right up front. The cost must be counted before anyone declares himself a Christian. Before a man or woman can claim the saving power of Jesus, they must count the cost demanded for salvation.

To merely believe and confess with your mouth that Jesus is Lord without matching action creates demonic faith that perverts the following Scripture.

For it is with your heart that you believe and are justified, and it is with your mouth that you confess and are saved. (Romans 10:10)

After all, don't the demons meet the requirements preached in most churches? Do not demons believe God exists? Do not demons even confess that Jesus is the Holy One of God?[9] Of course they do. Therefore to quote only Romans 10:10 while ignoring the rest of God's Word makes one's faith equal to that of demons.

> You believe that there is one God. Good! Even the demons believe that—and shudder.
> (James 2:19)

You believe in God. Great, even the demons, who will be tortured in hell, believe in God. Your opinion about God means nothing, just as the demons' beliefs about God do not keep them from being demonic. In fact, the difference between men and demons is that demons at least "shudder." They know enough to fear God and by the time the majority of people find out that their beliefs are lifeless, they too will "shudder." Demons feel terrified as to what will happen to them and we should be too, unless we repent. Demons, as well as all who have not repented as God commands, will "shout[ed] at the top" of their "voices" pleading with God not to "torture" them.

> He shouted at the top of his voice, "What do you want with me, Jesus, Son of the Most High God? Swear to God that you won't torture me!"
> (Mark 5:7)

God has an "appointed time" to literally "torture" those with demonic faith based on selfish motives and sin.

> "What do you want with us, Son of God?" they
> shouted. "Have you come here to torture us before
> the appointed time?" (Matthew 8:29)

You can hear their voices and almost feel their fear of being tortured by God.[10] We do well to take a hard honest look at what we call faith in God.[11] Most confuse faith in God with their "opinion" about spiritual matters. Others think of faith as simply declaring that they have asked God to come into their life. First, only a "fool delights" in his opinions about God. So the next time you find yourself in a group, school, or Sunday school class where everyone gives their opinions about God, feel free to quote the following Scripture.

> A fool finds no pleasure in understanding but
> delights in airing his own opinions.
> (Proverbs 18:2)

Secondly, most have come to God by simply asking Him into their lives. Their belief is merely opinion expressed with conviction. In other words, they believe they have God because they asked Him to come into their life. This corruption of Romans 10:10 takes away the saltiness of Jesus' salvation message.

Demons love it when people preach Romans 10:10 to the exclusion of the rest of Scripture, for this is what made them demons. They rejected God's perfect plan for them in favor of their own opinions, wants, and desires. Satan told Eve this same old lie when he cast doubt on what God said. Satan still performs the same old trick of asking, "Did God really say this is the way to be saved?"[12]

Many people become increasingly demonic in the name of Jesus. They think the sole requirement is to just "believe" in God. Without obedience or "action," however, a person cannot be saved. Remember, the demons believe in God but have no good action and thus their faith cannot save them.

In short, godly faith equals action, and obedience with the Holy Spirit expresses honest faith.[13] On the other hand, faith without God's "action" is merely man's opinions worked out for his own selfish ends.

> In the same way, faith by itself, if it is not accompanied by action, is dead. (James 2:17)

Truths to Ponder, Beliefs to Examine

⸺⸺⸺ ❧ ⸺⸺⸺

- What is wrong with the "just believe and you're saved" teaching?

- What cost did you pay to become a Christian?

- In what ways did you discover the price higher than you thought?

CHAPTER 3

Large Crowds Traveling with Jesus

L arge crowds" attend church today and "large crowds" come to hear preachers talk about Jesus. "Large crowds" of people buy books, listen to sermon tapes, and talk about Bible issues. Many individuals attend Bible College and seminary to study about God. There are "large crowds" "traveling" with Jesus and yet not a single one of them will go to heaven. Mere "travelers" will burn in hell forever.

Large crowds were traveling . . . (Luke 14:25)

We must understand the difference between a true Christian and a traveler following Jesus. A traveler comes along for the ride, enjoying the free food, miracles, and blessings of Jesus, yet they reject His way of salvation. They remain belly believers, and their faith always strives to get something from God.

> Their destiny is destruction, their god is their stomach, and their glory is in their shame. Their mind is on earthly things. (Philippians 3:19)

Travelers who follow Jesus to get something from Him should take warning. Jesus seeks to tell us "the truth" about ourselves; that we follow Him only because He will meet our selfish needs. Many want to eat "the loaves" and have their "fill" of peace, prosperity, happiness, blessings, and hope but refuse to fall in love with Him.

> Jesus answered, "I tell you the truth, you are looking for me, not because you saw miraculous signs but because you ate the loaves and had your fill." (John 6:26)

People prove their belly belief true when they reject the cross, God's way of saving a man. They follow Jesus, but have little interest in the cross, except that Jesus died for them. The church today contains multitudes of "travelers." Many consider themselves strong Christians, but they are mere travelers, not true disciples of Jesus. Jesus turned to these "large crowds" of travelers and spoke of the seriousness of calling oneself a Christian.

> Large crowds were traveling with Jesus, and turning to them he said: . . . (Luke 14:25)

The truth is, Jesus wasn't trying to make anyone a Christian; rather, Jesus came and died to make disciples. We will see the importance of this later on. For now, let us listen to Jesus as He speaks of God's salvation call or God's way of saving individuals. Man wants to entertain and make it easy to accept Jesus, while God tests and drives away all unworthy of eternal life.[14] Jesus' ways are for "anyone" who desires salvation. Jesus is emphatic about this.

If anyone comes . . . (Luke 14:26)

And anyone . . . (Luke 14:27)

Jesus spent over three years getting people ready for Peter's sermon at Pentecost. We, however, declare individuals to be Christians without ever preparing them. The church's interest in numbers motivates leaders to declare a new birth before conception has barely taken place. Paul compares Christ coming into a person's life to that of the process of child-birth,[15] but in our fleshly zeal we skip the suffering of pregnancy and delivery in order to justify our own sin. Wouldn't you think it strange for a husband to shout, "Come see my baby" if his wife was only one month along?

God spent thousands of years getting things ready for Jesus to come and preach the good news. Why then do we think someone is saved when we have to teach them the words to say in their own salvation prayer?

Jesus tested and tried people; He made them think, ponder, and become frustrated concerning the things of God in order to test their hunger for God.[16]

Like spoiled children whose parents anticipate and fill their every possible desire, we make salvation simple. We give people all the answers and make it easy for them to accept our version of Christianity, but we are not saving their souls.

As a result, we label mere travelers following Jesus as saved Christians, when nothing could be further from the truth. In our day the message of counting the cost is met with outright hostility because we have so cheapened the grace of God. What will you do? Will you change from a "traveler" to a "disciple?"

Truths to Ponder, Beliefs to Examine

- Who do you think the "large crowds" are today? Why do they follow Jesus?

- Explain the difference between a true follower and a traveler with Jesus.

- In what aspects of your life do you think you merely travel with Jesus? List some things you could do to become a follower.

CHAPTER 4

Christian or Disciple?

The man who loves his life will lose it, while the
man who hates his life in this world will keep it
for eternal life. (John 12:25)

Jesus hated His life while He walked on this earth. He
hated His life and carried His cross. The message
of hating one's life is the good news[17] Jesus preached
and lived. Only this message saves a man from hell
and honestly blesses his life. Without this hatred
Jesus says no one will gain "eternal life."

Many think that Jesus' teaching about hating
is not for young believers or for those considering
becoming a Christian. They wrongly believe that
somehow presenting this tough message up front
will only scare people away. But it was not so with
Jesus, for He was always blunt about the cross. He
remained upfront and bold about the requirements

of becoming a Christian. Jesus never said the Christian life would be easy.[18]

Jesus never put out a simple salvation call asking individuals to come forward if they wanted to be saved. Jesus never told crowds to raise their hands and just ask Him into their heart. Scripture never records anyone just asking Jesus into their heart by reciting a canned "believer's prayer." In fact, you will not find most modern methods of receiving salvation in the Bible. More specifically, today's methods of coming to the Lord hardly shadow what Jesus had in mind.

In the first place, Jesus did not come to make Christians, but disciples. This is an important distinction, mainly because when someone refers to themselves as a Christian they consider it a done deal. But Jesus looked at it differently. He sought to make disciples, and a disciple is someone in the act of continually learning from God. Even Jesus "learned obedience from what he suffered." Jesus, as the Son of Man, was the perfect disciple in whose steps we must follow.[19]

> Although he was a son, he learned obedience from what he suffered. (Hebrews 5:8)

Becoming a disciple demands a degree of humility and teachability that being a Christian does not require. A Christian sounds like a finished deal.

Think of a student in medical school learning what will make him a doctor. Not until graduation day can he call himself a doctor. So too, we will not really be Christians, people fully made in the image of Jesus, until we graduate and see Him "face to face."[20]

Even in the world, anyone desiring to become a physician must consider the cost to see if they are willing to pay the price to finish school. Just like the medical profession, many drop out and fall away from Jesus.[21]

Worldly non-believers first called disciples of Jesus "Christians."[22] The pagan world used this derogatory term while true believers of Jesus always referred to themselves as "disciples."[23]

The word "disciple" means a student, learner, or pupil. A disciple is in the process of being saved and waits for God's "coming of salvation," "revealed in the last time."[24]

> . . . who through faith are shielded by God's power until the coming of the salvation that is ready to be revealed in the last time.
> (1 Peter 1:5)

Jesus' salvation call speaks only of making "disciples." In the great commission of Matthew 28:19, Jesus does not say go make Christians; He bids us instead to go make "disciples." All through Luke 14:25–35, Jesus declares that if we do not agree to these things we cannot be a disciple. Only a disciple receives salvation.

. . . he cannot be my disciple. (Luke 14:26)

. . . cannot be my disciple. (Luke 14:27)

. . . cannot be my disciple. (Luke 14:33)

So Jesus poses the questions, "Are you willing to become a disciple? Are you willing to pay the price to be disciplined and become a disciple to the very end of your life?" Before you say "Yes," Jesus wants you to "sit down" and think about your decision.

Truths to Ponder, Beliefs to Examine

- Jesus "learned" obedience to God through suffering. What kinds of suffering do you think God puts a disciple through?

- Why do we need to continually learn from God? What might happen if we stopped learning?

- Sit down and ask yourself, "Am I willing to suffer to become a disciple?"

CHAPTER 5

First Sit Down

Will he not first sit down . . . ~Jesus

Jesus did not say, "Come on down to the front of the church and accept Me as your personal Lord and Savior." Jesus did not say, "Come get your blessing." Nor did Jesus apply rules to your life in order to receive salvation from hell. Jesus said that anyone even remotely thinking about becoming a Christian must first "sit down and estimate the cost."

He said, "sit down" and consider very carefully what it means to follow Him. Without emotional fanfare, Jesus calls all who desire His salvation to "sit down" and do some very sober thinking. Jesus never worked the crowds in order to gain followers, rather He always called for them to quietly "sit down" and "estimate" the cost of being saved. "Suppose one of you wants to build a tower . . ." and just "suppose one of you wants to" be a disciple . . . then "sit down."

> Suppose one of you wants to build a tower. Will he not first sit down and estimate the cost to see if he has enough money to complete it? For if he lays the foundation and is not able to finish it, everyone who sees it will ridicule him, saying, "This fellow began to build and was not able to finish." (Luke 14:28–30)

Many did not count the cost of laying a "foundation" only later to quit. Therefore do not take lightly Jesus' words about counting the cost. If those who did count the cost later decided it was not worth finishing the tower, then how much more should you, with sober thought, consider what it will cost you? Sad to say, many are "ridicule[d]" today because they counted the cost but later became unwilling to pay the price for full redemption from sin. Indeed, the next passage reveals that many of Jesus' "disciples," not mere travelers, left because the crucified life became too much for them.

> From this time many of his disciples turned back and no longer followed him. (John 6:66)

Many might think this all sounds like salvation by works and an attempt to earn God's salvation. But truthfully, Jesus declared that in order to receive God's free mercy, we must let go of all. Those who whine that this is salvation by works miss the whole point. Disciples simply respond to God's mercy everyday. Like "rain" that falls on good soil, it produces a "useful crop."[25] If the soil becomes hard, nothing of value can grow.[26] If a man hardens his heart, cutting off the power of grace, he will forfeit eternal life.[27] A disciple simply says "Yes" to the grace of God every day. This is the test, to say "Yes" to God at all times out of love for Him. If we do that, God can keep us from falling. God will never, however, force a man to be saved if he is unwilling to allow grace to flow through him.[28] If we refuse the grace that crucifies self, then we will be cut off, "thrown away," and eventually "burned" in hell.[29]

No man who truly wants to be rid of the sins in his life considers this a cost at all. "In his joy" the true disciple sells "all" to buy the "treasure" of God's grace and mercy. In short, it only sounds hard and legalistic to the hard-hearted. For only the hard-hearted and hard-headed refuse to give up all in exchange for a "treasure."

> The kingdom of heaven is like treasure hidden in a field. When a man found it, he hid it again, and then in his joy went and sold all he had and bought that field. (Matthew 13:44)

The treasure of Jesus is "hidden." God doesn't give knowledge about the message of the cross to everyone. It is too valuable and powerful for God to let the wicked trample upon it. Many religious churchgoers never find this treasure. While many who do find it never go back to it because they didn't "sit down" and think about the matter between themselves and God. They lose the treasure through confusion.

Once a man finds this treasure, he conceals it or keeps it to himself. Indeed, he hides it again, so that others are not aware of why he is selling everything. He becomes very quiet, contemplating alone what he has found between himself and God.[30] Unlike so many who go out to find opinion after opinion about what others think about Jesus, this man realizes the value and ponders it between himself and God. Those with bad hearts go from person to person, book to book exposing the treasure to the evaluation of men. They take before sinful man that which the Holy Spirit has opened their eyes to. They treat the treasure of grace as if it were a trinket found in the sand on a beach. How sad to watch so many, as God points them to the treasure, go out and become thoroughly confused as to whether Jesus, or the message of the cross, really is of God. Finally in their confusion they give up and refuse to dig up again the treasure they found earlier. The treasure became tarnished by man's hands, voices, commentaries, and watering down the gospel. Those who will not "sit down," with the treasure of God hidden again, will never find eternal life. It is "good" for a man or woman, when they discover the message of the cross, to "wait quietly for the salvation of the Lord."

The Lord is good to those whose hope is in him,
to the one who seeks him; it is good to wait quietly for the salvation of the Lord.
(Lamentations 3:25–26)

Truths to Ponder, Beliefs to Examine

• What would you consider the "treasures" of God?

• In what ways do you find waiting for God difficult?

side even while their lives remain loaded down with sinfulness. Multitudes of preachers and pastors preach a false message that God has forgiven them without repentance and obedience to God's way of salvation.[34]

While it is true that God loves us, it is also true that right now God prepares to judge the world and to send the vast majority of individuals, whether in the church or outside it, to hell. His just judgment comes and those not at peace with Him will be tortured in hell forever and ever.[35] This is why God tells us to "make every effort" to be saved.[36]

Let's examine how a man comes to peace with a God who is at war with him. What "terms of peace" does Jesus command us to "sit down" and think about?

> Or suppose a king is about to go to war against another king. Will he not first sit down and consider whether he is able with ten thousand men to oppose the one coming against him with twenty thousand? If he is not able, he will send a delegation while the other is still a long way off and will ask for terms of peace.
> (Luke 14:31–32)

Again Jesus says, "First sit down and consider" what it means to obtain "peace" with God. It is not just a matter of a simple salvation call, speaking in tongues, or asking Jesus in your heart. Indeed, experiencing miracles does not signify that a person is saved.[37] Only those who have sat down, counted the cost, and paid the price, travel the road of salvation.[38]

Since none can pay the price for their sins, we should, while God stays a "long way off" from condemning us, ask for His "terms of peace." Don't ask for your church's terms of peace, nor listen to your opinion about this matter. Get to know God's "terms of peace" and how to accept them, for He leaves no margin for error in this matter.

Join a "delegation" that moves out to meet God on His terms before the judgment day and surrender all. That is, find a church that understands and lives these "terms of peace." And when you find one, join them in their "effort" to be "found spotless, blameless, and at peace with" God.

> So then, dear friends, since you are looking forward to this, make every effort to be found spotless, blameless and at peace with him.
> (2 Peter 3:14)

Do you really think you can "oppose" God's army? How many foolishly believe their opinion about Scripture will change God's mind? How foolish to fight against God by thinking that discipleship is not required for salvation. Our logical gymnastics will not impede God's judgment from marching forward by a single step. A church's empty definition of grace will not succeed against God's army and survive the battle. It is a war lost before it begins, to try and water down God's way of salvation. Better to fully surrender to God and receive His blessings, than raise one argument that will forfeit paradise.

Truths to Ponder, Beliefs to Examine

—— ✺ ——

- Describe perfect peace.

- What sins in your life do you think God may oppose right now?

- Sit down in prayer and ask God for His terms of peace in your life.

CHAPTER 7

Losing Our Saltiness

Jesus said only the church that understands His salvation call remains "salty." If any church or disciple loses this "salty" quality of God's "terms of peace" it will be "thrown out." It drives one to tears to consider how many different styles of salvation calls will be "thrown out" in the end. The large numbers of individuals supposedly coming to Christ will prove to be the Church's shame,[39] because they rejected Jesus' salvation call and made up one of their own.

> Salt is good, but if it loses its saltiness, how can it be made salty again? It is fit neither for the soil nor for the manure pile; it is thrown out. "He who has ears to hear, let him hear."
> (Luke 14:34–35)

All those souls being "saved" will be "thrown out" because churches remove counting the cost from their messages. At our own peril, we ignore or change Jesus' salvation call.

The cost of salvation by Jesus is one-hundred-percent. It cost Jesus all to die for our sins, and as a fair exchange, we give Him everything.[40] All preaching to potential converts should involve estimating the cost. If not, the result is a wide gate[41] gospel call that many enter through to their destruction in hell. Jesus flat out declares, without shame, that it will cost a man everything in this world to be saved.

> In the same way, any of you who does not give up everything he has cannot be my disciple. (Luke 14:33)

Again, remember this is the starting point of what it means to be a Christian or a true disciple. This is not the end goal, but the requirement of entering the race of righteousness.[42] Anyone not willing to pay the entrance fee becomes disqualified right from the start. After all, a runner refusing to race "according to the rules" is disqualified from the prize. How many run the race toward God, but not "according to the rules!"[43] In the end, they find themselves disqualified for eternal life.

> Similarly, if anyone competes as an athlete, he
> does not receive the victor's crown unless he
> competes according to the rules.
> (2 Timothy 2:5)

This may sound like someone trying to earn his or her way to heaven. The schemes of man have altered the meaning of true faith in Jesus. When men speak of faith in the church today they falsely believe no matter what people do, if they believe in Jesus, they will go to heaven. That type of faith, without obedience, mocks Jesus' death. Jesus suffered, labored, and died to give us faith that works "obedience" in us.

> Through him and for his name's sake, we received
> grace and apostleship to call people from among
> all the Gentiles to the *obedience that comes from
> faith*. (Romans 1:5 emphasis added)

As the Scripture above reveals, Paul preached "grace" that produces "obedience." So true faith in Jesus starts and ends with obedience.[44] This means doing what God commands, in God's power, and in the way God declares things should be done. Without this true faith, our belief equals that of the demons'.

Truths to Ponder, Beliefs to Examine

———— ❧ ————

- Think of the qualities of salt. It gives flavor, it stings if poured on a wound, and it preserves and protects against germs and bacteria. With this in mind, describe a "salty" church.

- Do you think the church today as a whole fits this description? Why or why not?

- List a few of God's rules for running the race of salvation.

CHAPTER 8

Shaking the Salt Shaker

L et us shake the salt shaker just a little and see what a man or woman should consider before calling themselves a disciple of Jesus. The terms of peace, the cost of having true faith in Jesus, are threefold. We each have sinned against the God who is One, but manifested in three in the Trinity, so our repentance is threefold. First, we must hate those around us. Second, we must hate our own life. And third, we must pick up a cross and follow Jesus.

> Large crowds were traveling with Jesus, and turning to them he said: "If anyone comes to me and does not hate his father and mother, his wife and children, his brothers and sisters—yes, even his own life—he cannot be my disciple. And anyone who does not carry his cross and follow me cannot be my disciple." (Luke 14:25–27)

Of course this is not a worldly kind of hate that seeks to do harm to others. Yes, God is love and He desires that we love others.[45] However, we can only love God and others by "hating" and carrying our cross as we follow Jesus.[46] The following list shows just a few things to consider before you make your decision to follow Jesus. Please keep in mind these are only a few things that you should consider long before calling yourself a Christian.

- A complete rejection of all that is sinful.

> Aim for perfection . . .
> (2 Corinthians 13:11)

- A despising and hating of money.

> No servant can serve two masters. Either he will hate the one and love the other, or he will be devoted to the one and despise the other. You cannot serve both God and Money. (Luke 16:13)

- A total focus only upon the will of God.

> Why, you do not even know what will happen tomorrow. What is your life? You are a mist that appears for a little while and then vanishes. Instead, you ought to say, "If it is

the Lord's will, we will live and do this or that." (James 4:14–15)

- A willingness to have all pride put to death.

   The Lord is good to those whose hope is in him, to the one who seeks him; it is good to wait quietly for the salvation of the Lord. It is good for a man to bear the yoke while he is young. Let him sit alone in silence, for the Lord has laid it on him. Let him bury his face in the dust—there may yet be hope. Let him offer his cheek to one who would strike him, and let him be filled with disgrace. (Lamentations 3:25–30)

- An utter rejection of one's opinions and thoughts.

   A fool finds no pleasure in understanding but delights in airing his own opinions. (Proverbs 18:2)

- A new way of doing everything in daily life.

   So from now on we regard no one from a worldly point of view. Though we once regarded Christ in this way, we do so no longer. (2 Corinthians 5:16)

- A hatred of one's time, rest, comfort, fun, and joys.

  > The man who loves his life will lose it, while the man who hates his life in this world will keep it for eternal life. (John 12:25)

- Let God transform you into a slave.

  > . . . and whoever wants to be first must be slave of all. (Mark 10:44)

- Prepare for the possibility that there will be great division in your family.

  > Do you think I came to bring peace on earth? No, I tell you, but division. From now on there will be five in one family divided against each other, three against two and two against three. They will be divided, father against son and son against father, mother against daughter and daughter against mother, mother-in-law against daughter-in-law and daughter-in-law against mother-in-law. (Luke 12:51–53)

- Burn all your bridges to the life you now live.

  > Jesus replied, "No one who puts his hand to the plow and looks back is fit for service in the kingdom of God." (Luke 9:62)

- Be ready for the whole world to hate you.

  All men will hate you because of me, but he who stands firm to the end will be saved. (Mark 13:13)

- You could easily lose your job and reputation.

  They were stoned; they were sawed in two; they were put to death by the sword. They went about in sheepskins and goatskins, destitute, persecuted and mistreated—the world was not worthy of them. They wandered in deserts and mountains, and in caves and holes in the ground. (Hebrews 11:37–38)

- If you join a church truly of the Lord, you will be falsely accused of belonging to a cult.

  "We have found this man to be a troublemaker, stirring up riots among the Jews all over the world. He is a ringleader of the Nazarene sect . . ." (word "sect" is the same as cult). (Acts 24:5)

- Die having made yourself poor for others.

  For you know the grace of our Lord Jesus Christ, that though he was rich, yet for your sakes he became poor, so that you through his poverty might become rich. (2 Corinthians 8:9)

- A complete rejection of the ways of the world.

  > Do not conform any longer to the pattern of this world, but be transformed by the renewing of your mind. Then you will be able to test and approve what God's will is—his good, pleasing and perfect will. (Romans 12:2)

- A complete rejection of the things of the world.

  > Do not love the world or anything in the world. If anyone loves the world, the love of the Father is not in him. For everything in the world—the cravings of sinful man, the lust of his eyes and the boasting of what he has and does—comes not from the Father but from the world. The world and its desires pass away, but the man who does the will of God lives forever. (1 John 2:15–17)

- A willingness to be persecuted for Jesus.

  > In fact, everyone who wants to live a godly life in Christ Jesus will be persecuted, . . . (2 Timothy 3:12)

- A perseverance to suffer against sin until you are dead to sin.[47]

  > But the seed on good soil stands for those with a noble and good heart, who hear the

word, retain it, and by persevering produce
a crop. (Luke 8:15)

- A complete rejection of a good self-esteem.

    I know that nothing good lives in me, that
    is, in my sinful nature. For I have the desire
    to do what is good, but I cannot carry it out.
    (Romans 7:18)

- A resolve to do God's will no matter what family,
  friends, wife, brothers, or sisters say about that
  will.

    If anyone comes to me and does not hate his
    father and mother, his wife and children, his
    brothers and sisters—yes, even his own life—
    he cannot be my disciple. (Luke 14:26)

- A realization that God regretted making you.

    The Lord was grieved that he had made man
    on the earth, and his heart was filled with
    pain. (Genesis 6:6)

- A sense of weakness, of being unable to live the
  Christian life.

    That is why, for Christ's sake, I delight in
    weaknesses, in insults, in hardships, in

persecutions, in difficulties. For when I am
weak, then I am strong.
(2 Corinthians 12:10)

- An absolute surrender and death to every aspect
of self.

  For the sinful nature desires what is contrary
  to the Spirit, and the Spirit what is contrary
  to the sinful nature. They are in conflict with
  each other, so that you do not do what you
  want. (Galatians 5:17)

- No attachment to anything in the world.

  On that day no one who is on the roof of his
  house, with his goods inside, should go down
  to get them. Likewise, no one in the field
  should go back for anything. Remember Lot's
  wife! Whoever tries to keep his life will lose
  it, and whoever loses his life will preserve it.
  (Luke 17:31–33)

- To work out your salvation with fear and trembling, knowing you could lose it.[48]

  Therefore, my dear friends, as you have always obeyed—not only in my presence, but
  now much more in my absence—continue
  to work out your salvation with fear and
  trembling. (Philippians 2:12)

- A resolve, if married, to live as though not married.

  > What I mean, brothers, is that the time is short. From now on those who have wives should live as if they had none. (1 Corinthians 7:29)

- To not look for a wife or husband if unmarried, but to wait on God.

  > Are you married? Do not seek a divorce. Are you unmarried? Do not look for a wife. (1 Corinthians 7:27)

- To pray all of the time.

  > . . . pray continually . . . (1 Thessalonians 5:17)

- To be devoted to church.

  > Be devoted to one another in brotherly love. Honor one another above yourselves. (Romans 12:10)

- Be prepared to stop associating with anyone who claims to be a Christian but is a hypocrite.

  > But now I am writing you that you must not associate with anyone who calls himself a

> brother but is sexually immoral or greedy,
> an idolater or a slanderer, a drunkard or a
> swindler. With such a man do not even eat.
> (1 Corinthians 5:11)

• Come into the Light where your whole life is open before God and the church.

> But if we walk in the light, as he is in the
> light, we have fellowship with one another,
> and the blood of Jesus, his Son, purifies us
> from all sin. (1 John 1:7)

Are you willing for these things and more to be worked in your life by the power of God? Once a man or woman willingly strives to do only God's will, then comes the actual obedience by picking up the cross and following Jesus. Do you see why everyone must be a disciple? Just as Jesus carried His cross until He died on that cross, we cannot hope for a resurrected life without first carrying the cross the Holy Spirit gives us.[49] The apostles of Jesus gave up all and taught others the same.

> Peter said to him, "We have left everything to
> follow you!" (Mark 10:28)

To "follow" Jesus requires that everyone leave "everything" behind. Only those who hate their lives surrender all. Only those who surrender will let the cross crucify them to the world.[50] And only those who allow themselves to be crucified unto death experience the resurrected life.

Truths to Ponder, Beliefs to Examine

———————— ⌘ ————————

- Read back over the list in this chapter. Highlight or checkmark the things you see you need to do in your life.

- Ask God for the strength of His Spirit to be crucified with Christ.

CHAPTER 9

Why the Cross?

You should not be surprised at my saying, "You must be born again." (John 3:7)

We should not be "surprised" that we must be "born again." We are so totally worthless, vile, and corrupt that a brand new person must be created. Like the demons, we are completely undone, and we are like them in every way. The only difference between a demon and a man is that man has a choice. He can choose to be born again or refuse that chance. Demons had their chance in heaven and their opportunity has long passed. Hope does not exist in hell and there will be none for those who are not born again according to God's Word. As Paul declares, we are "worthless" and there is no one who "does good, not even one."

> All have turned away, they have together become worthless; there is no one who does good, not even one. (Romans 3:12)

We must fully realize and be convinced by God, through the cross, who we really are.

- We are rebellious, turning away from God.
- We have become totally worthless.
- We are unable to do a single good thing.
- There is not even one person who honestly looks for God.

Apart from Jesus man does not have one good thing about him.[51] Apart from being born again not a single ounce of good dwells in a person. Paul goes on to declare the facts of who we are and the reason we must be born again.

> Their throats are open graves; their tongues practice deceit. The poison of vipers is on their lips. Their mouths are full of cursing and bitterness. Their feet are swift to shed blood; ruin and misery mark their ways, and the way of peace they do not know. There is no fear of God before their eyes. (Romans 3:13–18)

Look at your life and then look again at what Romans declares. Surely if you look honestly you will see that you are all these things and more:

- Throat is an open grave.
- Tongue practices deceit.
- The poison of vipers is on your lips.
- Mouth is full of cursing and bitterness.
- Feet are swift to shed blood.
- Ruin and misery mark your ways.
- The way of peace you do not know.
- There is no fear of God before your eyes.

Without conviction from the Holy Spirit and acceptance of these facts, a man never submits to God's way of salvation, for he always feels unjustly accused. God's grace requires full surrender of all pride and self-justification, for God is "grieved" that he made you. As He looks at your life and what you have become "pain" fills His heart.

> The Lord saw how great man's wickedness on the earth had become, and that every inclination of the thoughts of his heart was only evil all the time. The Lord was grieved that he had made man on the earth, and his heart was filled with pain. (Genesis 6:5–6)

As has been said, we are wicked to the core and God came to send all to hell who love being bad. God's only solution is to start over with you. A completely new you must be created. A new you conformed to Jesus' image, righteousness, and holiness. Jesus didn't die so you could clean up your life a bit.[52] God isn't going to patch you up to keep your life happy. God is not like a doctor or psychiatrist who seeks to hold you together, knowing full well it will soon all fall apart.

You remain beyond hope of ever doing anything good in your current state, so God must start over. That is what it means to be born again. A complete new life starts and grows into adulthood over time.[53] Growth requires a cross in your life that will slowly kill the old you, thus making room for the new you to grow.

The cross, however, must continue its work. When a man or woman stops carrying the cross, the new life God created starts to die because the old you begins to take over again. If this situation continues long enough, the new life God started totally dies and the person becomes more fit for hell than when God first started. Better that he never even started trying to be a Christian.[54]

Disciples carry their cross "daily"[55] and prepare themselves for death to self upon that cross. The "message of the cross" truly delivers a man from sin. As Paul declares, "it is the power of God" for those "being saved."

> For the message of the cross is foolishness to those who are perishing, but to us who are being saved it is the power of God.
> (1 Corinthians 1:18)

Those who wish to rely on a simple, cheap grace salvation message are not actually "being saved." Only those embracing the "message of the cross" are "being saved," for that is where the "power of God" dwells.

Truths to Ponder, Beliefs to Examine

———————— ✑ ————————

- What obstacles have you faced in the struggle to "be good enough?"

- How does it make you feel to read in Romans that you have become worthless?

- What areas in your life do you still feel have worth? Embrace the cross and allow Christ to crucify these things.

CHAPTER 10

The First Sermon

If someone decides to pay the cost, how then does he become a Christian? How does someone begin the process of being crucified to self? What does it really mean to believe in the Lord or to accept Jesus Christ as your personal Lord and Savior? Correct answers to these questions grant anyone a brand new life if he comes to God with faith. Answering correctly allows one to discover how to be "saved." For answers we need to look no further than the very first sermon Peter preached after Jesus' resurrection from the dead. All preachers and churches should imitate this model sermon if they want to present God's grace correctly.

> "Therefore let all Israel be assured of this: God has made this Jesus, whom you crucified, both Lord and Christ." When the people heard this,

they were cut to the heart and said to Peter and the other apostles, "Brothers, what shall we do?" Peter replied, "Repent and be baptized, every one of you, in the name of Jesus Christ for the forgiveness of your sins. And you will receive the gift of the Holy Spirit. The promise is for you and your children and for all who are far off—for all whom the Lord our God will call." With many other words he warned them; and he pleaded with them, "Save yourselves from this corrupt generation." (Acts 2:36–40)

God shows that baptism is the next salvation step for those who have counted the cost. All the elements of Luke 14 are present in Peter's salvation sermon.

• The message of the cross is clearly presented. Because they knew Jesus' life,[56] they understood what the cross would mean for their lives.

Therefore let all Israel be assured of this: God has made this Jesus, whom you crucified, both Lord and Christ. (verse 36)

• Deep conviction over their utter sinfulness came over them. They were "cut to the heart," about who they were before God. This was no intellectual understanding or selfish desire to be blessed by God. They knew they were enemies and the terms of peace were complete surrender of everything.

. . . they were cut to the heart . . . (verse 37)

- They asked how to be saved and were broken and humble enough to accept God's way of righteousness. They did not argue or complain and look for some other way to ask Jesus into their life.

"Brothers, what shall we do?" (verse 37)

All who "accepted" Peter's message, which was really God's offer of mercy, were baptized. Those who would not accept what Peter preached, forfeited eternal life in heaven.

Those who accepted his message were baptized, and about three thousand were added to their number that day. (Acts 2:41)

They did not, as today, come forward and ask Jesus in their hearts, speak in tongues, or raise their hand and mock[57] back a prayer recited by the preacher. They were not so arrogant as to devise another way to salvation. Yet many will strive to discount the rest of Scripture by quoting Paul when he stated that God did not send him to baptize (1 Cor. 1:17). This is a staggering argument since Paul himself was baptized to "wash" "away" [his] "sins."

Paul understood that God declared that the way a man washes away the sins in his life is through the cleansing waters of baptism. How can a man say his sins have been washed away, when he has not been washed?

> And now what are you waiting for [Paul]? Get up, be baptized and wash your sins away, calling on his name. (Acts 22:16)

In 1 Corinthians 1:17, Paul means that baptism is not to be used as some prideful act to gain followers. People quickly started saying, "I follow Paul" versus some other person.[58] It is natural for man's sinful nature to boast in whom they follow, and who wouldn't take some secret pride in being baptized by Paul? Jesus Himself did not baptize just for this reason, but He taught His disciples to baptize.[59] It wasn't that Paul did not baptize, he was just "thankful" he didn't in Corinth so that no one would fall into boasting. Indeed, Paul baptized Lydia and it was only after her baptism that she was able to "persuade[d]" them she was a "believer in the Lord."

> One of those listening was a woman named Lydia, a dealer in purple cloth from the city of Thyatira, who was a worshiper of God. The Lord opened her heart to respond to Paul's message. When she and the members of her household were baptized, she invited us to her

home. "If you consider me a believer in the Lord," she said, "come and stay at my house." And she persuaded us. (Acts 16:14–15)

Notice that Paul baptized the jailer in Acts 16:33 and mature believers in Acts 19:5. Paul did not say that he never baptized. The point was that he personally did not baptize particular individuals because they might become puffed up in pride. To quote Paul, "I am thankful that I did not baptize any of you except Crispus and Gaius, *so no one can say that you were baptized into my name.*"[60] (emphasis added)

Paul and the apostles humbly submitted to God's righteous plan of saving man. They baptized in the name of the Father, Son, and Holy Spirit.[61] Preaching the complete and "full message"[62] caused everything to come together at once. They received the Holy Spirit, grace, mercy, and all the fullness of what it means to be saved all at one time. They did not complain that Peter made this salvation by works, therefore God could work His salvation in them.[63] Indeed, Peter later preached in the book of 1 Peter that "this water" saved them. To put it in his words, "this water symbolizes baptism that now saves you."

> . . . and this water symbolizes baptism that now saves you also—not the removal of dirt from the body but the pledge of a good conscience toward

> God. It saves you by the resurrection of Jesus
> Christ, . . . (1 Peter 3:21)

Note well that water baptism receives its saving power from the "resurrection of Jesus Christ." Those who complain about it argue against Jesus being raised from the dead. In other words, the faith of Romans 10:10 comes alive for the first time through water baptism.[64] For only as we believe in our "heart and confess with our mouth that Jesus is Lord" will we have the kind of faith that can save us through water baptism.

Truths to Ponder, Beliefs to Examine

- What elements of repentance were set in place in the believer's hearts in the book of Acts?

- Did anyone teach you about baptism?
  What were you told?

- How does that stand up to 1 Peter 3:21?

CHAPTER 11

The Full Message

But someone will say, "You have faith; I have deeds." Show me your faith without deeds, and I will show you my faith by what I do. (James 2:18)

Every Christian church and group requires certain "actions" that must be performed in order to receive salvation. Most groups say to just ask Jesus into your heart, others raise their hands, and some mock back a prayer. While some groups resort to a shallow application of water baptism, others mix it all up with speaking in tongues. Exactly what "action" does God have in mind for us to be saved? To put it in the words of the Scripture above, what does God require us to "do" in order to be saved? Let us look at the "full message" of God's good news.

> "Go, stand in the temple courts," he said, "and
> tell the people the full message of this new life."
> (Acts 5:20)

Peter preached a "full message" of the "new life" in Jesus and was told to do so by an angel of the Lord. Everyone should stand in the "temple courts," fully out in the open preaching the "full message."

Teaching the "full message" of God's grace means that the "Spirit, the water, and the blood" are taught at the same time, for the three totally agree. No one aspect is more or less important than the other. The water cleanses the conscience, the blood signifies the cost of the cross, and the Spirit gives everything true faith and life. Correct preaching declares all three.

The book of Romans only declares a requirement of "baptism." It doesn't specify if that baptism is water, Spirit, or blood because it is all one baptism. The blood is just as important as the Spirit and the water is just as important as the blood and the Spirit.

> For there are three that testify: the Spirit, the water
> and the blood; and the three are in agreement.
> (1 John 5:7–8)

Individuals and churches that would not consider leaving the blood or Spirit of Jesus out of their gospel calls have no qualms about leaving out the water. Let this sin no longer continue. These three things, because God is Triune in nature, testify to the unity of the message of the cross. When teaching is out of balance, God's people become hindered, walk in darkness, and are destroyed. In order to experience the resurrected life we must have all three aspects of Jesus. Why? First, because no one can get to God "except through" Him. Second, "the way" of the cross in Jesus is God's method of salvation. And third, this is the only way to "the life" of abundance in God.

> Jesus answered, "I am the way and the truth and the life. No one comes to the Father except through me." (John 14:6)

Jesus comes to each of us and asks us to accept all of Him, to believe in every aspect of who He is and what He stands for. Jesus is Truth and those who love Christ worship all of Him. For this reason John states that Jesus "came by water and blood." John knew that all of Jesus was of equal importance and power. Truly the Spirit, blood, and water are all required for salvation. Every aspect of the Truth is necessary if we want to walk victorious in this world and arrive safely at heaven's gates.[65] The Holy Spirit "testifies" to this Truth.

> This is the one who came by water and blood— Jesus Christ. He did not come by water only,

> but by water and blood. And it is the Spirit who
> testifies, because the Spirit is the truth.
> (1 John 5:6)

In order for a man to be "born again," he must first see the need to be born again. He must utterly abhor himself and admit the need for the cross in his life. When a man sees this clearly and has counted the cost, he is ready to be born again through the waters of baptism by the power of the Holy Spirit and the blood of the Lamb. Jesus taught this lesson through Nicodemus, by teaching a man must be baptized in "water and the Spirit" in order to be born again. Even natural birth demonstrates that the water and spirit are necessary. For there must be a spirit within a baby for there to be life, yet water surrounds the baby in the womb. Jesus uses the evidence of billions and billions of births to drive home the point that God's way of salvation comes through baptism.

As we will see in John 3:6, "flesh gives birth to flesh, but the Spirit gives birth to spirit." Both have their way of giving birth. Jesus teaches Nicodemus the way of the Spirit is through baptism. For "unless he is born of water and the Spirit" he cannot be born again. Nicodemus understood fully that Jesus was not talking about human birth, going back into the "womb," but about how to be born again by the power of the Holy Spirit.

Now there was a man of the Pharisees named Nicodemus, a member of the Jewish ruling council. He came to Jesus at night and said, "Rabbi, we know you are a teacher who has come from God. For no one could perform the miraculous signs you are doing if God were not with him." In reply Jesus declared, "I tell you the truth, no one can see the kingdom of God unless he is born again." "How can a man be born when he is old?" Nicodemus asked. "Surely he cannot enter a second time into his mother's womb to be born!" Jesus answered, "I tell you the truth, no one can enter the kingdom of God unless he is born of water and the Spirit. Flesh gives birth to flesh, but the Spirit gives birth to spirit. You should not be surprised at my saying, 'You must be born again.'" (John 3:1–7)

Man cannot be born again by saying a prayer, speaking in tongues, attending classes, or any other works man might devise. After all, is baptism more "works" than a prayer? Of course not; being baptized or saying a prayer to be saved both involve "doing" something. Therefore, doing something is a moot point. The only question is what did God command us to do in order to be saved? God did not tell us to speak a prayer to gain salvation. He declared that a man must be "born of water and the Spirit" in order to be born again. Among many, in an effort to make easy the grace of God, they have forgotten that Jesus also "came by water" as well as by "blood."

> This is the one who came by water and blood—Jesus Christ. He did not come by water only, but by water and blood. And it is the Spirit who testifies, because the Spirit is the truth. (1 John 5:6)

Truths to Ponder, Beliefs to Examine

- In what ways does the description of baptism in this chapter surprise you?

- What parts of the "full message" were you never taught?

- Meditate on the truth of 1 John 5:6. Have you been truly born again?

CHAPTER 12

Giving Orders

God demands that action and faith work together. Indeed, faith without action is not faith at all in God's sight. The book of James drives home the point by asking the following question:

> You foolish man, do you want evidence that faith without deeds is useless? (James 2:20)

This isn't earning salvation, rather it allows the salvation power of God to work and will in us.[66] Many stop the grace of God from producing works in them because of their stubborn hearts or bad teaching. For them, grace is without effect.[67]

While this publication cannot possibly refute every objection that stubborn hearts pose, let us at least answer the question of the thief on the cross. Some question if baptism of water, blood, and Spirit are required for salvation how could the thief on the cross go to heaven?[68] Look at the heart of God for the answer.[69]

Obviously if one cannot find water, or circumstances prevent baptism, they will be saved.[70] God sees the heart and knows His children.[71] However, if people's hearts truly love God, they gladly obey all of God's commands for the reasons God declares, as soon as the opportunity presents itself.[72] Consider well, that if Jesus did not exempt Himself from baptism, even though He did not need to be baptized, under what justification do you excuse yourself?[73]

Know this; even if you think you have the Holy Spirit, you still must be water baptized for salvation. Indeed, you are "ordered" to be water baptized for the reasons God states.

> "Can anyone keep these people from being baptized with water? They have received the Holy Spirit just as we have." So he *ordered* that they be baptized in the name of Jesus Christ. Then they asked Peter to stay with them for a few days. (Acts 10:47–48 emphasis added)

As we look deeper at the meaning of water baptism, we can destroy another excuse or question, "What if I were in the desert? What then?" Of course God works and wills to provide in every situation.[74] For if God is powerful enough to give us a way out when tempted,[75] He can certainly make a way for us to be righteous. Just look at the following true incident. Let us follow Philip on the "desert road" and see what happened. Note well it was a "desert road," a place where one could go miles without even a hint of water to drink, let alone enough to be immersed or baptized.[76]

> Now an angel of the Lord said to Philip, "Go south to the road—the desert road—that goes down from Jerusalem to Gaza." (Acts 8:26)

The Ethiopian eunuch's story begins by studying the book of Isaiah and ends with water baptism. Philip begins "with that very passage of Scripture" and concludes with water baptism. So it should be with us. As we talk about the Holy Spirit, grace, mercy, or any other passage of Scripture with an unbeliever, we should end with water baptism. If we preach the true "good news about Jesus" we will end where Philip ended, standing in water.

> Then Philip began with that very passage of Scripture and told him the good news about Jesus. As they traveled along the road, they came to some water and the eunuch said, "Look, here is water. Why shouldn't I be baptized?" And he gave orders to stop the chariot. Then both Philip and the eunuch went down into the water and Philip baptized him. When they came up out of the water, the Spirit of the Lord suddenly took Philip away, and the eunuch did not see him

again, but went on his way rejoicing. Philip, however, appeared at Azotus and traveled about, preaching the gospel in all the towns until he reached Caesarea. (Act 8:35–40)

"Look, here is water," the eunuch exclaimed. Somehow, from the preaching of Philip, the eunuch came to a correct conclusion about how to be saved. In his determination the eunuch gave "orders" for the chariot to stop so he could be water baptized. The God who controls the universe and arranges where men should live[77] knew that this exact moment required water. Even in a desert, God can work and will His full message of salvation if the heart willingly responds to God's grace.[78] With tender hearts "both Philip and the eunuch went down into the water" to baptize the eunuch. Coming "up out of the water," they each went the way of God's will as disciples of Jesus.

Truths to Ponder, Beliefs to Examine

- What questions or arguments arise in your mind about baptism?

- How does the story of the Ethiopian eunuch answer these doubts?

- Why did the eunuch go on his way rejoicing? Does this knowledge of baptism cause you to rejoice? Why or why not?

CHAPTER 13

A Daily Cross

The cross kills the very essence of who you are and destroys your very self and life, while God creates a totally new you. When this happens, God gives you a new self, made in the image of Jesus to replace the one crucified unto death. Water baptism begins the process. God plants the seed of new life in you at baptism. And as the old dies, the new comes to life each day.[79] The same book in the Bible that speaks of confessing with our mouths and believing in our hearts, tells us how to be "freed from sin." Paul tells us baptism is the key.

> What shall we say, then? Shall we go on sinning so that grace may increase? By no means! We died to sin; how can we live in it any longer? Or don't you know that all of us who were baptized into Christ Jesus were baptized into his death? We were therefore buried with him through

baptism into death in order that, just as Christ was raised from the dead through the glory of the Father, we too may live a new life. If we have been united with him like this in his death, we will certainly also be united with him in his resurrection. For we know that our old self was crucified with him so that the body of sin might be done away with, that we should no longer be slaves to sin—because anyone who has died has been freed from sin. (Romans 6:1–7)

A man dies to sin by being "buried" with Christ "into death" so that God can give him a "new life." Apart from this call to baptism, little of the true resurrected life exists. For no man can "know that" his "old self was crucified" if he has not been "united with him *like this* in his death" (emphasis added). This is one reason why infant baptism is completely rejected. There is no way for babies to understand what happens to them, nor have an opportunity to count the cost to recognize themselves as sinners[80] and obtain faith from God.[81]

Going under the water symbolizes entering the tomb with Jesus and dying to ourselves. Coming "up" out of the water represents a resurrected person in the image of Jesus, just as Jesus was resurrected up out of the tomb.

A man can ask Jesus into his heart all day long, but without this baptism the "old self" has not been crucified and put to death. Would you like to no longer be a slave to sin? Then submit to God's righteousness instead of trying to establish and live by your church's doctrine or personal opinion.

During water baptism, a man or woman picks up the cross that comes from Jesus for the very first time. Men and women in churches throughout the world pick up crosses to carry, but that does not mean Jesus chose those crosses for them.[82] This is why Jesus ended with saying, "and follow me." Without following Jesus the cross they carry has no power to save, deliver, or change them. A man must pick up a daily cross if he expects the salvation of God in his life. In order for the saving grace to enter a man's soul, there must spring to life deep denial of self that has the cross as its central focus unto a resurrected life.[83]

> Then he said to them all: "If anyone would come after me, he must deny himself and take up his cross daily and follow me." (Luke 9:23)

It is the daily cross that causes us to mature in Jesus. Without this daily crucifixion the new self withers and slowly dies.[84] So slow that the person doesn't even notice they are falling away.[85] For this reason, Peter urged us to make sure we grow up in our faith. If we refuse to "make" our "calling and election sure" then we will "fall."

> Therefore, my brothers, be all the more eager to
> make your calling and election sure. For if you
> do these things, you will never fall, and you will
> receive a rich welcome into the eternal kingdom
> of our Lord and Savior Jesus Christ.
> (2 Peter 1:10–11)

Like babies, Peter urges new believers to "crave
pure spiritual milk."[86] Carrying a daily cross allows
the Word of God to mature us and to make us strong.
Those who "daily" are crucified to a little bit more
self "will receive a rich welcome into the eternal
kingdom" of Jesus.

Truths to Ponder, Beliefs to Examine

———— ✍ ————

- How can someone die daily?

- What sins in your life do you need to bury with Christ?

- Describe the cross Christ has in your life.

Having This Attitude

The new life begins, but God desires for us to go on to maturity.[87] Indeed, only those who produce a good crop in maturity will be found worthy of eternal life.[88] Just as every good parent desires for their child to grow up and display good qualities, so too God desires the same in our lives.[89] For this reason, we need to carry our cross daily to grow.[90] The question begs itself, are you willing to carry your cross daily and suffer against sin in order to overcome?[91] For God's Word tells us only those who "overcome"[92] reside in heaven with Jesus. Listen to the preaching of Peter again about the cross in a disciple's life.

> Therefore, since Christ suffered in his body, arm yourselves also with the same attitude, because he who has suffered in his body is done with sin. As a result, he does not live the rest of his earthly

life for evil human desires, but rather for the will of God. (1 Peter 4:1–2)

When Jesus was crucified on the cross, He felt the pain of nails in His hands and feet. He agonized as death came by inches and slowly over hours. Indeed, He suffered humiliation as they whipped, beat, and terrorized Him before making Him carry the cross outside Jerusalem. Dying on the cross became a very real physical matter for Jesus. It was no intellectual religious mind exercise, but rather suffering death combined with spiritual turmoil and battle. Peter encourages us to obtain this "same attitude," because only those who have "suffered" in their bodies are "done with sin." Only those who "suffer," feeling in their bodies in a very physical way the power of the cross, can walk the new life in Jesus.

The resurrected life happens only as a "result" of suffering by the power of the cross with sin. Very few churches have experienced this cleansing power from blood shed on a cross. Fellowship in the Light in a church that understands the power of suffering with Jesus causes the "blood of Jesus" to purify "us from all sin."

But if we walk in the light, as he is in the light, we have fellowship with one another, and the blood of Jesus, his Son, purifies us from all sin. (1 John 1:7)

A person can only do God's will by suffering against sin because the flesh must be dealt with first. Most just do not want that kind of saving grace and turn to the multitude of self-help books, deliverance ministries, support groups, and revival meetings that dot the land. It is much easier to talk about sin than to suffer in one's body. It is simpler to pray with everyone about problems than to suffer and die on the cross over them. As a result, the church embraces many other ways to deal with sin other than the cross. Few want to suffer enough on the cross against sin to be dead to it. Most remain selfishly content and lazy to just let Jesus do all the suffering for them. They do not love Him enough to suffer with Him.

To preach or live anything less than this message is to live a lie. If we desire to experience the life-changing power of God every day, we must also share equally in the suffering of the cross. As Paul joyously declares, "we always carry around in our body the death of Jesus, so that the life of Jesus" may be in us. If you are willing to "always" have the death of Jesus working in you then you can expect His powerful life to also reside in you.

> We always carry around in our body the death of Jesus, so that the life of Jesus may also be revealed in our body. (2 Corinthians 4:10)

The true Holy Spirit-inspired Christian walk shares in the sufferings of Jesus. In other words, no one really enjoys the comforts of Jesus if we do not have His sufferings flowing into our lives. The vast majority of church goers experience the false salvation, one without the sufferings of Christ. They have a comfort, but it will only last in this world. A disciple's "comfort overflows" in his life because the "sufferings of Christ" also fill his life.

> For just as the sufferings of Christ flow over into our lives, so also through Christ our comfort overflows. (2 Corinthians 1:5)

Any preaching or life lived differently than this supports false Christianity. Only those who "share in the sufferings" of Christ on an hourly basis can claim the title of true "children" of God. No one is an "heir" of the good things to come unless they "indeed" suffer in their bodies with and against sin.

> Now if we are children, then we are heirs—heirs of God and co-heirs with Christ, if indeed we share in his sufferings in order that we may also share in his glory. (Romans 8:17)

If you desire the "glory" of God that overcomes sin, then you must share in the sufferings of Christ. If you are willing to pay the price, then begin today by being crucified to yourself and God will give you the beginnings of a new life.

Quick fixes for our sin do not exist. No wide gate or road leads to salvation. Instead, we must enter through a narrow gate and walk a narrow road to heaven. Jesus said only a "few find it" while "many" enter through the wide gate of just asking Jesus in their heart, to their destruction.

> Enter through the narrow gate. For wide is the gate and broad is the road that leads to destruction, and many enter through it. But small is the gate and narrow the road that leads to life, and only a few find it. (Matthew 7:13–14)

Again, are you willing to pay the cost for such a life of discipleship? Do you really hate sin and wickedness enough to give it all up so that God's righteousness may remain in you? If so, plant this attitude in your heart and mind by the power of the Holy Spirit. Many do not really want the power to overcome sin. They love the flesh and sinfulness too much. They have no real desire to be made well and would rather spend their time making excuses as to why they have not changed.[93] God will give you the power to live all of this, it is simply a matter of whether you really want to be a disciple.[94]

Truths to Ponder, Beliefs to Examine

— ❧ —

• Describe Jesus' attitude in suffering on the cross.

• Explain how you can have the same attitude.

• What steps can you take to enter the narrow gate?

CHAPTER 15

Re-Baptized

Often people state, "I don't know if my baptism was valid or not," as they begin to understand the true meaning of baptism. It is a good question because most have been taught a very superficial teaching about baptism, while many others were baptized with mixed motives and doctrines. Still others feel they have been Christians for years without baptism. For answers to these questions and concerns, let's look at the baptism of John the Baptist, for he came preaching with baptism in mind.

> And so John came, baptizing in the desert region and preaching a baptism of repentance for the forgiveness of sins. (Mark 1:4)

John preached a powerful and life-changing message that offered "the forgiveness of sins." Yet,

John said that his baptism could not compare to the baptism Jesus would bring.

> And this was his message: "After me will come one more powerful than I, the thongs of whose sandals I am not worthy to stoop down and untie. I baptize you with water, but he will baptize you with the Holy Spirit." (Mark 1:7-8)

Note that while John was sent by God, he, unlike many other preachers today, realized that he preached an inferior baptism. Many individuals confuse this type of baptism as a salvation baptism. They often point to their changed lives and claim others should acknowledge their salvation because of these changes. John's preaching and baptism, however, also produced many changed lives, but still remained incomparable to the baptism of Jesus. Those who refuse to humble themselves and acknowledge their need for true baptism are in dangerous disobedience. Remember many rejected Jesus because they had not been baptized by John. In the same way, many refuse to move onto maturity and cling falsely to their first convictions of God as assurance of salvation.[95]

Unlike John the Baptist, many preach their church dogma and baptize with impure motives. For instance, the desire for numbers and the rushing of children into baptism to reassure parents simply reveals two sins committed in the name of baptism.

Such polluting of God's way of salvation forces many to conclude later in life that their baptism was not of God.[96] For most, however, baptism is a matter of tradition, something done to them as a baby or to prove their faith, or worse yet to join a church. Since God does not delight in ignorance, it is imperative that all repent and be baptized for the correct reasons and by the power of the Holy Spirit.[97] The vast majority baptized were not dipped by the pure working of the Holy Spirit but by the mixed and sinful workings of religious man. Although individuals might say they gave themselves to God, it is very proper to ask if the Holy Spirit prompted them, with sufficient wisdom from God, or did the motivation of men urge them into the baptismal waters.

In our preaching and discipleship, let us, as the Holy Spirit gives insight, enable others to see the baptism of John they underwent. In no way am I advocating a new or added baptism, but a call for spiritual wisdom. Simply stated, the first convictions and changes in one's life toward God may constitute the baptism of John. Those first stirrings may well be on the level of John's message. Therefore, we must fully teach the complete message of Jesus and make certain that all count the cost, testing to make sure of the Holy Spirit's presence, before we pronounce anyone born again. So many teachers, preachers, and Christians only know the power of John's message and therefore completely lack the greater power of the baptism of Jesus. They may be accurate and full of zeal, good hearted, and loving toward God, but have a greater need of understanding and power. The following example is one such preacher who humbled himself and was richly blessed for it. Though knowing Jesus "accurately," this man remained in need of spiritual growth because he "knew only the baptism of John." Once again Scripture reveals God's desire that the salvation message should be consistent among all churches and individuals. If a particular message lacks the full knowledge of salvation, something must be added.

> Meanwhile a Jew named Apollos, a native of Alexandria, came to Ephesus. He was a learned man, with a thorough knowledge of the Scriptures. He had been instructed in the way of the Lord, and he spoke with great fervor and taught about Jesus accurately, though he knew only the baptism of John. He began to speak boldly in the synagogue. When Priscilla and Aquila heard him, they invited him to their home and explained to him the way of God more adequately.[98]

For many this book will "more adequately" help them understand, preach, obey, and experience Jesus Christ and His salvation message. Yet, many others will reject this and in self-righteousness may lose the grace God began. Hopefully a few will humble themselves and find a grace they never dreamed possible.

Let us end this chapter with another quick look at the baptism of John. The baptism and repentance of John is simply this; changing everything humanly possible through the outward touches of God's grace. This baptism fills in the valleys of self-pity, relaxation, and worldly pleasures so the person can focus in on heavenly matters. Such a person stops enjoying the weekend and reads the Bible on Saturday to prepare for church on Sunday. It is going to John in the desert, away from all the entertainment, commerce, and food of this world to hear the rough, clear, offensive Word of God preached. For most readers this book presents their first encounter with the desert preaching of John because the churches they attend are too defiled to proclaim the offense of the cross.[99] You will not often hear a "voice of one crying in the desert" from pulpits today. John's baptism inspires a life of preparation; of getting up early to read the Bible, turning off the TV, avoiding friends of bad influence, and looking for things that crowd out God. First step of denying self: Do not look for a church that pleases self.

John's message shows things you can do to make straight your crooked life. Whether opinions about God or everyday little things that make it hard for Jesus to reach you, this baptism causes you to throw them away.

The wise in the Lord will direct such repentant sinners into a proper position so that God can touch them. Those already wise in Jesus, but only knowing the baptism of John, can lay hold of even more in Christ. The unwise and hard hearted, however, will angrily reject this message and grow bitter that they are called to give up even more—indeed, their very selves. Prepare your heart for God to draw closer to you and if you discover the need to be baptized again, humbly submit and "all mankind will see God's salvation."

> . . . during the high priesthood of Annas and Caiaphas, the word of God came to John son of Zechariah in the desert. He went into all the country around the Jordan, preaching a baptism of repentance for the forgiveness of sins. As is written in the book of the words of Isaiah the prophet: "A voice of one calling in the desert, 'Prepare the way for the Lord, make straight paths for him. Every valley shall be filled in, every mountain and hill made low. The crooked roads shall become straight, the rough ways smooth. And all mankind will see God's salvation.'"
> (Luke 3:2-6)

Truths to Ponder, Beliefs to Examine

———— ∽ ————

• Explain the significance of the baptism of John.

• What areas in your life do you need more power?

• Prayerfully examine your baptism or lack of. Ask God to reveal if you participated in the baptism of John or the Spirit.

CHAPTER 16

The Joy

"Where is the joy?" is an objection often voiced
about the message of the cross. I am always
surprised at the question because the forgiveness of
sins and the ability to pursue righteousness by God's
grace should cause joy to spring from our hearts.
Sadly, it is not enough in today's worldly church.

As we have seen, this joy is not like the world
and it is ever before us until it reaches its fullness in
heaven. In other words, the joy that comes from the
Holy Spirit increases as we allow the cross to crucify
our sinful nature. The worldly naturally desire a
joy like the world, a joy that is fleshly, unspiritual,
and quickly gained. The kind of joy God offers us
is the kind He gave His Son; therefore we are called
to "fix our eyes on Jesus." If we gaze upon Jesus we
will notice the joy is "set before" us only as we have
"endured the cross." Any other kind of joy comes

from Satan and is the desire of evil men who may
or may not claim to be saved by God.

> Let us fix our eyes on Jesus, the author and
> perfecter of our faith, who for the joy set before
> him endured the cross, scorning its shame, and
> sat down at the right hand of the throne of God.
> (Hebrews 12:2)

Worldly people desire feelings of joy, but God
gives us the "shame" of the cross so He can bless
us by turning us from our sins (Acts 3:26). We feel
shame over our sins, but find hope in Christ, life
by death to self, and a taste of glory while we are
hard pressed in this world. We know there is no
condemnation but should not be so foolish as to
believe there is no conviction. The wondrous joy
of Jesus is so completely unlike the world that the
worldly in and out of the church often marvel at
a true disciples joy in Jesus. They simply cannot
understand why we would have joy.

> We are hard pressed on every side, but not
> crushed; perplexed, but not in despair; perse-
> cuted, but not abandoned; struck down, but not
> destroyed. We always carry around in our body
> the death of Jesus, so that the life of Jesus may
> also be revealed in our body.
> (2 Corinthians 4:8-10)

The worldly also desire a rest and peace from the struggle against sin, but God calls us in faithful obedience to suffer with His Son. Those unwilling to carry their daily cross will be found unworthy of salvation and blotted out of the book of life. Only after we have scorned the cross, that means to pour contempt on any whining about how rough, difficult, or narrow the cross makes life, will God allow us to sit down with Jesus in heaven. This is not salvation by works, whereby we earn our salvation, rather, we allow Jesus to not only "author" or start our faith, but to "perfect[er]" it as well. Many are satisfied that God authors their faith, but very often fall away when God seeks to perfect it. They are wicked, lazy servants who care nothing about righteousness, but in selfishness desire only to be filled with a joy so they can take more pleasure in their sins.

Does all of this mean that God leaves us joyless as we follow the Holy Spirit? In the words of Paul the Apostle, "by no means." The Holy Spirit filled Jesus, the man of sorrows, with joy, but He still endured much suffering and the cross lay ahead of Him. In short, He had a long road to walk before the resurrected life was granted.

At that time Jesus, full of joy through the Holy Spirit . . . (Luke 10:21)

As Romans 12 instructs, our minds must be transformed to understand all of this. For no worldly person can possibly understand the joy in the message of the cross. Such people remain unwilling to accept that the message of the cross is joy supreme in this world. Why? Because they love their sin more than the righteousness of God.

We might praise God, but not in the same way the deceived do, who fill their hearts with a fleshly kind of emotion. True Christians rejoice with a fear that causes them to tremble.

> Serve the LORD with fear and rejoice with trembling. (Psalm 2:11)

In experiencing passing joys and sorrows in the Lord we have hope that one day we will be filled with everlasting joy in the presence of God. Surrender to the work and will of God and let Him work the emotions each hour that He desires. With each old self emotion we are called to fall to the ground and die so that the Holy Spirit might work what we should feel at any given moment. Doing so will ensure that you persevere to the end as you carry your daily cross in faith through Jesus. What should you expect to feel after your baptism? "Pure joy" of course.

> Consider it pure joy, my brothers, whenever you face trials of many kinds, because you know that the testing of your faith develops perseverance.

> Perseverance must finish its work so that you
> may be mature and complete, not lacking any-
> thing. (James 1:2-4)

The Holy Spirit will seek to teach and work in you a pure joy in God that rejoices in facing many trials and testings. This is the way of the crucified life, and baptism provides the first step in the journey to pure joy.

Think of it this way; does a thief love a policeman and his message? Of course not, because it keeps him from doing what he loves to do, namely steal. In the same way many, though claiming to be Christians, react angrily at the true gospel call because it reveals they steal from Jesus. They steal His forgiveness while rejecting His righteousness. They want the forgiveness of Jesus poured into their lives, but will not allow the righteousness to be poured in as well because they would have to hate their own lives. Like a thief, they want the judge to forgive them so that they can continue to steal.

Paul tells us to "keep the Festival" of God. A festival means the celebration of righteousness. For those who love the righteousness of God it is the celebration or joy they participate in all year long. With this godly attitude every command becomes a new joy in Jesus. Every way of God becomes a joyful path to walk, and every promise of God, though it has the cross present, is celebrated. Joining such a church is going to a festival of righteousness. Every true Christian is marked by their eagerness to obey the Bible, walk in the ways of God, and above all, to love others.

> Therefore let us keep the Festival, not with the old yeast, the yeast of malice and wickedness, but with bread without yeast, the bread of sincerity and truth. (1 Corinthians 5:8)

Let us end with the question we started with, "Where is the joy?" It is not like the world, but only found as we pick up our cross and follow Jesus. It is found by not seeking joy as if it were our right or something to be held onto, but by only seeking the will and face of God. Joy in sorrow, hope in affliction, and the promise of eternal life as we die daily with Christ.

> . . . sorrowful, yet always rejoicing . . .
> (2 Corinthians 6:10)

The joy of Jesus is found by never letting go of the sorrow the cross produces. When this sorrow is rejected we end up with a joy like the world, hellish and demonic.

Truths to Ponder, Beliefs to Examine

- Describe what joy means to you. Think of the things that bring "joy" in your life.

- Explain how suffering and trials can produce joy.

- Does this concept of joy confuse you? Lift up to the Lord the areas in your life where you lack the true joy of righteousness.

CHAPTER 17

Why Become a Christian?

This is the verdict: Light has come into the world,
but men loved darkness instead of light because
their deeds were evil. Everyone who does evil
hates the light, and will not come into the light
for fear that his deeds will be exposed.
(John 3:19–20)

Whether you honestly want God's mercy and
grace can be answered with a very simple
question. Are you tired of a life in the darkness and
do you hunger for light? Jesus died for mankind to
allow those who hunger for holiness, truth, good-
ness, purity, and love a chance to possess these
qualities.[100] Those who hate evil come into the light
to become righteous like Jesus.[101] In short, there is
only one real reason why someone would want to
become a disciple.

You might be asking yourself, with all the suffering and loss involved in a Christian's life why would anyone want to be a disciple? The answer is very simple, yet few want it. It is a matter of loving God. True love for God is stronger than death, even death to self.[102] God is holy, perfect love[103] and those who desire God want to be with Him, and be like their Father.

Which Father do you want to be like? Those who do not love God this way belong to their "father, the devil" and want to do what pleases him and themselves. There is no middle ground, either it is the cross in a man's life or it is the devil in his life.

> You belong to your father, the devil, and you want
> to carry out your father's desire . . . (John 8:44)

Disciples love what is good, and God is very good. In fact, God is the only one good and in loving Him we love all that is good.[104] Only when we desire everything noble, right, pure, lovely, admirable, excellent, and praiseworthy can we expect the "God of peace" in our lives. God only loves and fellowships with those who love righteousness.[105] Those who come to Jesus just because their lives are miserable are in for a terrible shock on judgment day.[106]

> Finally, brothers, whatever is true, whatever is
> noble, whatever is right, whatever is pure, whatever is lovely, whatever is admirable—if anything

is excellent or praiseworthy—think about such things. Whatever you have learned or received or heard from me, or seen in me—put it into practice. And the God of peace will be with you. (Philippians 4:8–9)

Now is our time of "testing."[107] A man who loves God, loves righteousness, truth, and holiness no matter the suffering or loss.[108] Those who love wickedness want a false Jesus who will bless them in a worldly manner.[109] If you love God with a true desire, you consider the cross in your life a thing of beauty and joy. The cross forms a person into the image of Jesus and is God's method for making us ready for His holiness. Those dying to themselves are transformed into the likeness of Jesus and therefore sin gradually vanishes. A true Christian sins less and less each day. If you know someone who claims to be a Christian but is a hypocrite,[110] they are not really of Jesus. Because Jesus "appeared" to "take away our sins" so that a person will stop sinning.

But you know that he appeared so that he might take away our sins. And in him is no sin. No one who lives in him keeps on sinning. No one who continues to sin has either seen him or known him. (1 John 3:5–6)

Anyone who tells you they know God but continues to sin is a liar. Just like the demons who believe in God but keep on sinning, so too, such people have a demonic faith without the life-changing power of a crucifying cross. Don't "let anyone lead you astray" in this matter. Someone who honestly follows Jesus will stop sinning. A true disciple sees new sins to die to each day while they stop the old sins of the past from rising up. Indeed, they "cannot go on sinning, because" they have "been born of God."

> Dear children, do not let anyone lead you astray. He who does what is right is righteous, just as he is righteous. He who does what is sinful is of the devil, because the devil has been sinning from the beginning. The reason the Son of God appeared was to destroy the devil's work. No one who is born of God will continue to sin, because God's seed remains in him; he cannot go on sinning, because he has been born of God. (1 John 3:7–9)

If you do not find the cross to be a joy, the odds are you will persecute those who do follow Jesus on the narrow road.[111] Think about Moses who made a conscious choice to be "mistreated" with the "people of God rather than to enjoy the pleasures of sin for a short time." Admittedly, sin is fun and enjoyable, while the cross brings pain and crucifies us to the world. If someone portrays Christianity as fun and enjoyable, they preach a false Jesus.[112]

He chose to be mistreated along with the people
of God rather than to enjoy the pleasures of sin
for a short time. He regarded disgrace for the sake
of Christ as of greater value than the treasures
of Egypt, because he was looking ahead to his
reward. (Hebrews 11:25–26)

The cross gives us each a choice. If we "value"
the "treasures of Egypt"[113] more than the love of God,
we reject this message. Our acceptance or rejection
of the message of the cross reveals who and what
we love.

If you "hunger and thirst for righteousness," God
makes you into a brand new person so that your
righteousness results from His power.

Blessed are those who hunger and thirst for
righteousness, for they will be filled
(Matthew 5:6)

The salvation call of Jesus comes with true "au-
thority" and power.[114] His salvation call demands
we obey all He requires by the power of the Holy
Spirit through faith.[115] This is what God means by
"grace," it is His power in us to say "No" to sin.[116]
The good news of God grants us a "festival" of righteousness, denying self, and hating our lives in this
world.[117] The good news lets us obey God, having
our sins washed away, so that we can enjoy sweet
fellowship with Him.[118] God's amazing grace gives

us the power to become totally new creations.[119] Those who merely want the blessings of God apart from the crucified life use God to indulge themselves in their sinful desires. They are like demons who believe in God, yet are still demons by nature. Like devils, they want the things of God for their own ends, but are not in love with God's character. Those who honestly love God want to be like Jesus, and Jesus became who He was, as the Son of Man, by the cross manifested in His life. A true disciple lives for the hope of being "like him." If we really love Jesus then we will want to imitate Him while we are in "this world." Only with this message can we have "confidence" that our faith is ready for "the day of judgment."

> In this way, love is made complete among us so that we will have confidence on the day of judgment, because in this world we are like him. (1 John 4:17)

Truths to Ponder, Beliefs to Examine

- Define a true disciple of Christ.

- Did you ever think it possible to stop sinning?

- List some "little" sins in your life that you thought would never stop.

- Determine to place them at the cross one at a time.

CHAPTER 18

Feelings

Our first concern should not be with what we will feel. But what will God feel? Will He be well pleased with us as He was with His only begotten Son? Often people ask, "What should I expect to feel after I am baptized?" First and most importantly, baptism is not about feelings—it is about faith. Feelings come and go like waves tossing upon the seas, colliding upon each other. What we feel at one moment passes away in the next. Continue to sail the course of faith, ignoring the waves, and God will ensure you arrive safely at the shores of heaven.

God did, however, create us as different emotional beings, and what individuals experience at baptism will vary. While no one can speak completely for the will of God, looking to Jesus can help us catch a glimpse of what to expect.

In Acts 5:32 we saw that God only gives the Holy Spirit to those who "obey Him," so if you were baptized for the correct reasons you will sense God's pleasure with you in Christ. You will sense by faith that God poured forth His love upon you through Jesus. Remember by faith we are saved, so expect much mercy from God and you will sense His love. Do not measure your feelings by what others have felt. God will come to you in the loving way He has chosen for you. God's love is very personal and is granted to each person in His timing and way. Rest in faith that God loves you and is well pleased as you seek to fulfill all righteousness.

> As soon as Jesus was baptized, he went up out of the water. At that moment heaven was opened, and he saw the Spirit of God descending like a dove and lighting on him. And a voice from heaven said, "This is my Son, whom I love; with him I am well pleased." (Matthew 3:16-17)

Besides feeling wet, you may experience the immediate joy and lifting of the burden of guilt.[120] Just as Jesus was full of joy at the sight of seeing the Holy Spirit in the shape of a dove and hearing His Father's voice, so too a proper measure of God's love will be sensed by all who come to Him with an honest faith. Remember, one of the meanings of baptism is a pledge of a good conscience toward God. As you pick up your cross and do the will of

God each day, you will grow sensitive and convicted of sin and learn to quickly repent. Therefore you can expect many emotions and different feelings as you follow the Holy Spirit. The Spirit led Jesus into the desert to face confrontation by Satan right after His baptism. You, as a child of God, should expect a taste of the same experiences. For this reason God said to consider the rock from which you were cut (Isaiah 51:1).

> Then Jesus was led by the Spirit into the desert to be tempted by the devil. (Matthew 4:1)

Likewise, the Holy Spirit will lead you into the desert to face the attacks of the Evil One. Water baptism is not the finish line, but the starting line for the race of faith and new life. Out in the desert, with all of its discomforts, trials, and fears, the Spirit will lead you. God led the Israelites into the desert after their baptism, and in the desert we begin the fight of faith. God will seek to make you into the image of Jesus and so you can also expect to face the desert and then the crucifixion. Remember that the Bible compares the baptism of Jesus to fire and it far exceeds the baptism of John. Just think for a moment about the message John preached![121] You will be immersed with the Holy Spirit and fire. Most reject this refreshing water and cleansing fire that comes so powerfully against sin and instead turn to a worldly, religious baptism with no real power.

> John answered them all, "I baptize you with
> water. But one more powerful than I will come,
> the thongs of whose sandals I am not worthy to
> untie. He will baptize you with the Holy Spirit
> and with fire." (Luke 3:16)

Since this is a Christian's lot, don't expect your feelings of joy to resemble the world or what you are used to. You will become a new creation with a new understanding and sensations of joy never experienced before. You will learn true sorrow and true joy. Your joy, however, will not be like the world's so do not expect to be filled with over-flowing amounts of happy sensations. Those who seek such things fall prey to Satan's schemes and end up idolizing emotions. The joy in Jesus is "inexpressible." In other words, it is unlike the world in every way because it is a "glorious joy." Flesh cannot express or understand the joy found in Jesus, it is beyond the scope of human sorrow or happiness.

> Though you have not seen him, you love him;
> and even though you do not see him now, you
> believe in him and are filled with an inexpressible
> and glorious joy. (1 Peter 1:8)

Since the joy and peace Jesus gives does not resemble the world's, do not look for it in the way of the world or think that you will understand at first the true joy of Jesus (John 14:27). No tears of joy or sensations of excitement can possibly express the joy God desires to place in our hearts. It is a joy beyond our own hearts, for the emotions change almost with each beat.

> For God is greater than our hearts, and he knows everything. (1 John 3:20b)

Those baptized correctly have been buried and raised new creations through Christ. The born again individuals have fresh kinds of emotions that only the Holy Spirit can work. Like a new born baby, there is much to learn about what to feel in the Lord. They will experience days of rich emotional praise, ones of quiet silence, and days of sorrow and seriousness. The important thing is to prepare to persevere past the emotions. No matter what emotions fill your heart, your faith must rise above them all.

> If you do not stand firm in your faith, you will not stand at all. (Isaiah 7:9b)

Truths to Ponder, Beliefs to Examine

—⁓—

- What types of feelings do you base decisions or attitudes on?

- Describe the emotions or feelings of guilt you want lifted from your heart.

- Ask God to fill you with the emotions that come from His Holy Spirit.

The First Step
of Humility

> Then Philip ran up to the chariot and heard the
> man reading Isaiah the prophet. "Do you under-
> stand what you are reading?" Philip asked. "How
> can I," he said, "unless someone explains it to
> me?" So he invited Philip to come up and sit with
> him. (Acts 8:30–31)

D o you understand what you are reading?"
Be humble enough like the eunuch in the
story above to say, "How can I?" The cross crucifies
pride. Like the eunuch, find a true disciple of Jesus
to "invite[d]" into your life who can teach you to
count the cost and baptize you "in the name of the
Father, Son, and Holy Spirit." God will honor this,
and you will begin a new day, with a new life as a
disciple of Jesus. Ask God to send you someone who
understands what it means to count the cost, how
to suffer against sin, how to count suffering as a joy,

who denies self unto death, and knows how to really be born again. Find someone without a legalistic or shallow understanding of water baptism, but who themselves have walked through the narrow gate by the power of the Holy Spirit.[122]

Usually a person will think this is beyond them to live. They feel hopeless in attempting to live this kind of Christianity. Many voiced this very concern to Jesus and He simply told them to make "every effort."[123] The good news is that if you want to love God, He will give you His power to walk the narrow road.

The message of the cross is not a matter of a bunch of rules, principles, and applications of dos or don'ts. Rather it means surrendering to God to do the work through you.[124] So the question isn't whether you can live this kind of life, it is a question of whether you are willing to let Jesus honestly be Lord of your life. Only those who say it is "hopeless" to live this life will be given divine power to walk the narrow road.[125]

Pray for God to show you who preaches and lives the "full message." Many groups preach only the Spirit, (blessings, miracles, feelings) and therefore remove the blood (cost, suffering, testimonies) and these partial gospels can never deliver one from sin. Many others speak of only the blood, (cost, denying self) but do not have the Spirit (oil, joy) or the water (refreshment, purity) all of which leaves the believer despondent and weak. Still other groups preach the water of Jesus but forget the blood and the Spirit. For them Jesus is an intellectual or feel-good experience. Let God lead you to a church where you feel uncomfortable. After all, the cross is not a comfortable thing to hang on and a church preaching the complete message of the cross can feel very unsettling to join.[126] If you can't find someone with these basics down, realize that they offer you, at best, only part of the good news. After all, if the foundation is faulty there is a greater danger the house will collapse.[127]

The salvation call of Jesus includes the altar of sacrifice that will forever change a man. The old Law of the Bible required many sacrifices burnt on the altar for sins. Jesus completed the law by offering Himself as a sacrifice for our sins. Jesus lived a life continually sacrificing Himself to God. And those born again, in the image of Jesus, live a life of continual sacrifice to God. Disciples of Jesus walk in the footsteps of Jesus by daily offering their "bodies" as living sacrifices.

> Therefore, I urge you, brothers, in view of God's mercy, to offer your bodies as living sacrifices, holy and pleasing to God—this is your spiritual act of worship. (Romans 12:1)

A true "act of worship" towards God requires that a man or woman sacrifice themselves to God.

God's "mercy" motivates a thankful-hearted[128] person to become a disciple.[129] Without sacrificing everything to God, we have no hope of salvation.[130] Are you ready, with joy in your heart, to count the cost, pay the price, and become a disciple? If so the Scripture below is for you. If you desire to "obey everything" by the new self that God will create, then Jesus commands you to become a "disciple," by being baptized in the name of the Father, Son, and Holy Spirit. Then every day, as you grow in the Lord, confess with your mouth and believe in your heart that Jesus is Lord. Then your faith will be real and it will provide the blessing of saving your soul.

> Then Jesus came to them and said, "All authority in heaven and on earth has been given to me. Therefore go and make disciples of all nations, baptizing them in the name of the Father and of the Son and of the Holy Spirit, and teaching them to obey everything I have commanded you. And surely I am with you always, to the very end of the age." (Matthew 28:18–20)

What a blessing it is to know Jesus remains "always" with us "to the very end of the age." Those who obey God by faith have the right and the privilege to walk in this blessing.[131] As we have seen, God only gives the Holy Spirit to those who "obey him." Those who have true faith in God obey Him in this way, by the power of the Holy Spirit and for the reasons He commands. Faith gives the power to obey and the new life springs from obedience to God. Note well that God only gives the Holy Spirit to those who "obey him" day in and day out.

> We are witnesses of these things, and so is the Holy Spirit, whom God has given to those who *obey him*. (Acts 5:32 emphasis added)

It happens all by faith, but the new life is maintained and grows only as we obey the Holy Spirit with a living faith.[132] For a man who says he believes something but does not act with the power of that belief is as a demon. After all, "even the demons believe—and shudder."

Truths to Ponder, Beliefs to Examine

∾

- Describe the meaning of the term "full message."

- What parts of the full message do you want to lay hold of in your life? Ask God for the strength and humility to take that first step.

- What are you waiting for?

And now what are you waiting for? Get up, be baptized and wash your sins away, calling on his name. (Acts 22:16)

EVERYTHING SAID

With everything said, look to God whose ways can save you from cheap grace and never-ending death in hell.

───────────── ❦ ─────────────

For you have delivered me from death and my feet from stumbling, that I may walk before God in the light of life. (Psalm 56:13)

ENDNOTES

1. Peter 2:24 He himself bore our sins in his body on the tree, so that we might die to sins and live for righteousness; by his wounds you have been healed.
2. 1 Corinthians 1:12–13
3. Ephesians 6:24
4. Isaiah 26:10
5. 1 Corinthians 2:4
6. Luke 14:25–35 Large crowds were traveling with Jesus, and turning to them he said: "If anyone comes to me and does not hate his father and mother, his wife and children, his brothers and sisters—yes, even his own life—he cannot be my disciple. And anyone who does not carry his cross and follow me cannot be my disciple. Suppose one of you wants to build a tower. Will he not first sit down and estimate the cost to see if he has enough money to complete it? For if he lays the foundation and is not able to finish it, everyone who sees it will ridicule him, saying, 'This fellow began to build and was not able to finish.' Or suppose a king is about to go to war against another king. Will he not first sit down and consider whether he is able with ten thousand men to oppose the one coming

against him with twenty thousand? If he is not able, he will send a delegation while the other is still a long way off and will ask for terms of peace. In the same way, any of you who does not give up everything he has cannot be my disciple. Salt is good, but if it loses its saltiness, how can it be made salty again? It is fit neither for the soil nor for the manure pile; it is thrown out. He who has ears to hear, let him hear."

7. Psalm 49:13

8. Ecclesiastes 3:11

9. Mark 1:24

10. Hebrews 10:31

11. 2 Corinthians 13:5

12. Genesis 3:1

13. Galatians 5:6

14. Matthew 22:12

15. Galatians 4:19

16. Mark 10:21, Luke 9:59–62

17. Acts 14:22, note "many hardships."

18. John 16:33

19. 1 John 2:6

20. 1 Corinthians 13:12

21. Mark 4:17, Hebrews 6:6

22. Acts 11:26, literally "little Christ."

23. Acts 6:1, 6:7, 9:1, 9:19, 9:26, 18:23, 18:27, 19:1, 21:4–5

24. Disciples are individuals that were saved, are being saved and will be saved. Salvation, like discipleship, is a process. God has given us free choice and we can stop this process of saving grace and thus fall away, (Hebrews 6:4–8). Romans 10:10, 2 Corinthians 2:15, 1 Peter 1:5, 1 Corinthians 1:18, Ephesians 2:5, Philippians 1:28, 2 Timothy 1:9, Hebrews 9:28, 1 Thessalonians 5:8, Romans 8:24, Ephesians 1:13–14, Romans 13:11, Ephesians 1:4–5.

25. Hebrews 6:7

26. Hebrews 6:7–8

27. Hebrews 3:15

28. Jude 1:24

29. John 15:6

30. Lamentations 3:28

31. John 4:14

32. Isaiah 48:22

33. Revelation 6:12–17

34. Ezekiel 13:10–15

35. Revelation 14:11

36. 2 Peter 3:14

37. Matthew 7:22

38. Psalm 50:5

39. Philippians 3:19

40. Luke 17:33

41. Matthew 7:13

42. 2 Timothy 4:7

43. Matthew 22:12

44. Matthew 25:31–46

45. 1 John 4:16

46. *Hating for Jesus*, Timothy Williams (Enumclaw, WA: WinePress Publishing, 2000), ISBN 1-57921-646-3, or *A Whisper Revival—Our Only Option*, Timothy Williams (Enumclaw, WA: WinePress Publishing, 2000) ISBN 1-57921-274-3.

47. 1 Peter 4:1–2

48. Hebrews 6:6

49. Romans 8:13

50. Galatians 6:14

51. Proverbs 12:10, note: the "kindest acts of the wicked are cruel."

52. Matthew 12:43–44

53. 1 Peter 2:2

54. 2 Peter 2:21–22

55. Luke 9:23

56. John 12:32, Galatians 3:1

57. Proverbs 1:22

58. 1 Corinthians 1:12, 3:4

59. John 4:2, 1 Corinthians 1:12

60. 1 Corinthians 1:14–15 (emphasis added)

61. Matthew 28:19

62. Acts 5:20

63. John 6:65

64. Romans 10:10

65. Hosea 4:6

66. Acts 26:19, 1 Corinthians 15:10

67. 1 Corinthians 15:10

68. Luke 23:43 Jesus answered him, "I tell you the truth, today you will be with me in paradise."

69. Mark 2:27, note: For example, the Law demanded a Sabbath rest, but the law would be misunderstood if the heart of God was not taken into account.

70. Romans 2:25–29

71. 2 Timothy 2:19

72. Ephesians 5:15–16

73. Matthew 3:15

74. 1 Corinthians 10:13

75. 1 Corinthians 10:13

76. The word baptism means immersed.

77. Acts 17:26

78. Ephesians 1:11

79. 2 Corinthians 5:17

80. Psalm 51:5

81. John 6:44

82. John 21:22

83. Many will "heap abuse" on you for your life of denying self. Do not let them stop you from following Jesus. (1 Peter 4:4)

84. John 15:6

85. Revelation 3:1–2

86. 1 Peter 2:2

87. Hebrews 6:1, Hebrews 5:12

88. Luke 8:14–15

89. Hebrews 12:10

90. Luke 8:14

91. Hebrews 12:4

92. 1 John 5:5, Revelation 2:7, 2:11, 2:17, 2:26, 3:5, 3:12, 3:21, 21:7

93. Ezekiel 18:2–3, John 5:6

94. John 15:4–5

95. But the Pharisees and experts in the law rejected God's purpose for themselves, because they had not been baptized by John. (Luke 7:30)

    Therefore let us leave the elementary teachings about Christ and go on to maturity, not laying again the foundation of repentance from acts that lead to death, and of faith in God, (Hebrews 6:1)

    The path of the righteous is like the first gleam of dawn, shining ever brighter till the full light of day. (Proverbs 4:18)

96. Must my flock feed on what you have trampled and drink what you have muddied with your feet? (Ezekiel 34:19)

97. In the past God overlooked such ignorance, but now he commands all people everywhere to repent. (Acts 17:30)

98. Meanwhile a Jew named Apollos, a native of Alexandria, came to Ephesus. He was a learned man, with a thorough knowledge of the Scriptures. He had been instructed in the way of the Lord, and he spoke with great fervor and taught about Jesus accurately, though he knew only the baptism of John. He began to speak boldly in the synagogue. When Priscilla and Aquila heard him, they invited him to their home and explained to him the way of God more adequately. (Acts 18:24-26)

99. But mark this: There will be terrible times in the last days. People will be lovers of themselves, lovers of money, boastful, proud, abusive, disobedient to their parents, ungrateful, unholy, without love, unforgiving, slanderous, without self-control, brutal, not lovers of the good, treacherous, rash, conceited, lovers of pleasure rather than lovers of God-- having a form of godliness but denying its power. Have nothing to do with them. (2 Timothy 3:1-5)

100. Matthew 5:6

101. John 3:20–21

102. Song of Songs 8:6

103. 1 John 4:16

104. Mark 10:18

105. Daniel 9:4

106. Luke 17:17

107. Hebrews 3:8

108. Revelation 22:11–12

109. Psalm 17:14

110. 1 Corinthians 5:11

111. 2 Timothy 3:12

112. Galatians 6:14, 1 John 2:15, 2 Timothy 3:4, Micah 2:11

113. Egypt in the Bible symbolizes the world with all of its goods and pleasures.

114. Matthew 7:29

115. Matthew 28:20

116. Titus 2:12

117. 1 Corinthians 5:8

118. 1 Peter 3:21

119. Titus 2:12

120. Let us draw near to God with a sincere heart in full assurance of faith, having our hearts sprinkled to cleanse us from a guilty conscience and having our bodies washed with pure water. (Hebrews 10:22)

121. After John's messengers left, Jesus began to speak to the crowd about John: "What did you go out into the desert to see? A reed swayed by the wind? (Luke 7:24)

122. Matthew 7:13

123. Luke 13:23–24

124. Colossians 2:23

125. Isaiah 57:10

126. Acts 5:13

127. 1 Corinthians 3:10–14

128. 1 John 4:19

129. 1 John 4:19

130. Hebrews 9:22

131. Psalm 50:16

132. Romans 1:17

Other books written by Timothy Williams

Insanity in the Church
- *Insanity in the Church* addresses the specific lies the church now regards as truth, making it ripe for the Powerful Delusion of the end times. Find out the only cure to the Powerful Delusion.
- ISBN 1-57921-390-1

Hating for Jesus
- This book examines why Jesus said *anyone* who follows Him *must* hate his own life.
- ISBN 1-57921-646-3

A Whisper Revival
- This book explains how God wants to lead us to the "quiet waters" (Psalm 23:2) where we can honestly be revived.
- ISBN 1-57921-274-3

Love in the First Church
- This book explains the fruit of God's love being worked in a body of believers, and how many will consider that to look like a cult.
- ISBN 1-57921-511-4

To order additional copies of

EVEN
THE
DEMONS
BELIEVE

Call:

(360) 802-2550

Or write to us at:

Sound Doctrine Ministries
PO Box 856
Enumclaw, WA 98022
USA

Or visit our web site and on-line store at:

www.carriedcross.org

Special discount ministry and group rates
are available. Please call us.

For more information about becoming a disciple contact: